Crate Training Your Puppy:

Minimize Headaches and Accidents by Learning the Smartest Way to Train Your Puppy

D1569447

Kenneth Harrison

Table of Contents

Additionally, the information in the following pages is intended only for informational purposes and should thus be thought of as universal. As befitting its nature, it is presented without assurance regarding its prolonged validity or interim quality. Trademarks that are mentioned are done without written consent and can in no way be considered an endorsement from the trademark holder.

Introduction

Crate training instills the appropriate behaviors in a puppy. For instance, if he has a habit of chewing on things, through crate training, your puppy will only have his toys to chew on and resist the urge of chewing on your household items.

Through crate training, a puppy will have his behavior modified. During travels, it can be extremely difficult to handle your puppy if he is not crated.

Keep in mind that for your puppy to take a liking to his crate, you must introduce it in an acceptable way. If you force him into the crate, he will resent being held in there, and the exercise will not bear any fruit.

A crate trained puppy allows the owner to be able to leave for work, knowing that their puppy is safe and secure. This book details everything you need to know about crate training so that your puppy can have a smooth time assimilating into your life.

Chapter 1: The Basics of Crate training

Crate training is the process of introducing a crate to your dog and making them feel comfortable inside the crate. Most dog trainers consider it one of the most important tasks. Some of the reasons why people buy dog crates include:

- Toilet-training purposes
- Keeping your pet safe
- Establishing house rules
- Providing a place where your dog can feel at ease
- Acts as a unit for transporting your dog conveniently

Dogs love staying in dens. If you introduce the crate appropriately, your puppy will love it. Your puppy will run into it when they need to take a break from the house. In many instances, a puppy develops an attachment to their crate; they would even want to spend entire nights there.

Even if dogs are den-animals, if you take the wrong approach, they will resent the crates and possibly become scared of them. You need to exercise caution when crate training your dog.

Introduce the crate carefully

Never come home one day with a crate and force your puppy inside it. It will scare them. Dogs resent being forced into any kind of situation that is against their will.

The best approach is to make the crate seem like a fun piece of furniture. Place it around a part of the house that they enjoy spending time in.

Make the interior well decorated and then stand back and watch whether they will be curious enough to go in. Do not forget to praise your dog every time that they walk into the crate.

Putting snacks and toys in the crate will encourage the dog to walk in. You can also initiate games with your dog around the crate so that they warm up to the idea of getting inside.

You want your dog to perceive the crate as a place for having fun and not a prison.

Gradually, start issuing subtle commands to your dog, like instructing them to go into the crate. Reward them whenever they obey. If your dog looks scared, stay until they are comfortable. Never walk out and assume that they will get used to it.

Extend the stay

When the dog has gotten accustomed to climbing into the dog crate, the next challenge is to lengthen their stay. The intention is to create a positive notion about the crate, so that they may be able to stay in the crate for a long time without necessarily being checked on.

Setting up their meals inside the crate is a nifty way of ensuring a prolonged stay since the dog will eat and possibly take a nap, it will result in increasing their familiarity with the crate. Place the food towards the end of the crate, so that the dog will walk all the way in.

Closing the crate

Once your dog has become somewhat accustomed to life in the crate, you should start closing it. This ensures that your dog can stay for a long period of time inside the cage without needing any attention.

Slamming the door shut while your dog is resting on their paunches is likely to scare them. The best approach is to shut the door slowly whenever the dog is busy with a toy or feeding.

Initially, when you close the door the dog might whine, you should open it again and try to soothe their anxiety away by gently stroking him and then slowly close it again. With careful approach and persistence, your dog should soon adjust to having the door of the crate closed.

Next, you can walk off to see how the dog copes with your absence, but stay nearby just in case they have separation anxiety. Calm down their fears and encourage them to withstand your absence. Soon, the dog will not only be comfortable in the cage but also will take a liking to it.

Do not use the crate as a form of punishment

Some people tend to scoop their dog up when they have done a mistake and shove them into the crate. This causes the dog to develop negative feelings about the crate.

Moving on, it becomes hard to get your dog to ever want to be in the crate. If you want your dog to be happy about spending time in the crate, you should ensure that they have positive feelings about the crate.

Space

Ensure that the crate is large enough for the dog to move around. Depending on the size of the dog, you want to buy a crate that can accommodate them reasonably well, but not too large at the same time.

Safety

The crate might serve as your dog's haven when you are not around, and because of this, you want to ensure that the crate is as safe as could be. First off, ensure that there are no sharp edges, as they put your dog at risk of skin tear.

Ensure there are no spaces through which a predator could come in. Do not forget to take off the collar so that the dog may be free to move around.

Chapter 2: Why Should You Crate Train Your Puppy?

Crate training has been termed as one of the most important things to do for your dog. Some dog owners seem uncomfortable with the whole idea, at least initially. Here are some of the reasons why crate training your dog is considered important.

It is a safe haven

Dogs have it in their nature to stay in dens. When you consider the atmosphere of many homes, you can understand that from time to time your dog will need to pull away from all the activities and spend some alone time in a "den."

Having a dog crate serves this purpose. When your dog climbs into the crate, you should let them have some quality time on their own. This will lead to an emotionally gratified dog that will connect with you at an even deeper level. Also, the crate serves as a refuge to the dog whenever they face a threat.

Housetraining purposes

Dog owners get frustrated when their dog relieves themselves without paying attention to where they are. Crates are vital equipment, as they help you teach your dog how to control their bladder and bowel movement.

When you housetrain your dog, you must exercise patience and resist from punishing your dog when they fail to adhere to your rules. The whole exercise must hinge on patience and persistence. In the end, your dog will become disciplined enough to relieve himself where you want them to. After all, dogs hate dwelling in a soiled environment.

Safety

It can be nerve-wracking to go to work and leave your dog behind, imagining all the crazy things your dog might be up to. A dog crate provides a sanctuary for your dog.

This way, you can enclose the dog in the haven when you are not around. Also, when you are having a renovation in your house or cleaning it, you may keep the dog in the crate as it would be dangerous for them frolicking around, considering that sharp tools might harm them.

Fun

When you get your dog a crate, one of the things you must provide is a toy. This will ensure that the dog will have something to play with as the hours roll by.

When your dog has some toys in their crate, they can easily chew on those toys instead of other valuable things in your household like furniture. Also, crates are great for feeding your dog. Ideally, you should put the food toward the end. When you combine food and attractive toys, your dog will be very entertained.

Traveling

It can be quite hectic to move around when the dog is not restrained. For instance, it is convenient to have your dog in the crate when you are traveling by road, as opposed to them prancing around in the car, which would pose safety concerns.

A dog crate ensures that your dog is confined in a comfortable environment, in which they can function without facing constraints. The preparation encourages the dog to develop a positive feeling toward the crate so that eventually, they become attached to the crate and want to spend most of their time there.

Guests

Not to mean that guests are allergic to dogs, but for some reason, you might prefer to have the dog held away when your guests are around. If you lack a dog crate, you will not be able to do it without hurting your dog's feelings. A crate serves as a good place to put your dog when you have guests over.

Easier vet visits

Sometimes, the dog might come down with an illness that requires them to stay with the vet for more than a day. In such instances, it does the vet a world of good that the dog is crate trained. The dog will also be far more at peace in a new territory when they are confined in their crate.

For calming your dog

Some dogs can really escalate their feelings and actions. In such cases, a significant amount of damage is done. A crate is crucial for managing such dogs. You may put your dog in the crate as a way of calming them down. A crate trained dog responds well to time-outs.

Evacuation

As long as you live in a modern house, there are various potential disasters and emergencies. It is easier to evacuate a dog who has been crate trained than the one who is not. If your dog is handed over to new owners, the separation hurts them less because they are still in their own crate and surrounded by familiar items.

Chapter 3: Picking the Best Crate for Your Dog

A dog crate gives your dog his own personal space. There are several things to consider before selecting a dog crate: how you plan to use it, the age of your dog, their personality, and their breed.

The practical concerns include: how easy it is to clean and carry around, and whether the color and material of the crate align with your aesthetic taste.

Dog crates come in a wide range of sizes, styles, designs, and materials. All dog crates will hold your dog and help with potty training.

Picking the dog crate that is best for you will depend on the size of your dog and other variables. Here are some of the questions that you should ask yourself before you purchase a crate:

- Will the crate get moved around or will it stay in one place?
- Will you travel long distances with the crate?
- Does your dog have the habit of chewing on things?
- Will it be easy to clean up this crate?
- How does the crate fit into your home and decor?

The biggest mistake that most dog owners make is buying a crate that is a few sizes too big. Before you buy a crate, you should first measure the size of your dog.

To get their height, you should measure from the top of their shoulders to their paws; to get their length, you should measure from the tip of their nose to the tip of their tail. The ideal crate should allow your dog to stand up, sit down, and turn around comfortably. The door should be wide enough for the dog to go in and out without any difficulties.

These are the five basic types of dog crates:

1. **Plastic crates**
2. **Wire crates**
3. **Heavy-duty crates**

4. **Soft-sided crates**
5. **Cute crates**

1. Plastic crates

It takes two pieces of molded plastic to make this type of crate. The top and bottom are held in place by plastic fasteners, and there is a metal-wire door.

Some crates designed for puppies tend to have a plastic door which is a huge drawback, considering that puppies like chewing on things. Most plastic crates have a moat that runs around the edge of the floor which traps the dog's urine and drains it.

Advantages of plastic crates

- The space is comfortable
- Makes it easier to travel with your dog
- Good at containing puppies
- Available in different colors
- The top half can come off easily and get stacked with the bottom half for easier storage

Disadvantages of plastic crates

- On warm days, it can get hot in there
- It limits your dog's scope of vision which might disorient them

- Not very aesthetically pleasing

2. Wire dog crates

For the most part, these crates are made of panels of wire, but the floor is made of plastic. The material that is used is sturdy, and it also discourages the habit of chewing up things.

Advantages of wire crates

- It has great ventilation which allows dogs to be at ease. The wire crate is perhaps the best choice for dogs living in hot climates.
- You can section off the crate using a divider. This allows you to increase the area occupied by the dog as they grow older.
- It can be folded. This proves important when carrying or storing the crate.
- The removable floor makes it easy to clean.

Disadvantages of wire crates

- They produce more noise than plastic crates when your dog moves around
- Some models are weak enough for a dog to break free.
- The design is not attractive

3. Soft-sided crates

Soft-sided is considered the most portable crates. It is available in a wide range of styles, sizes, and materials.

Advantages of soft-sided crates

- It is lightweight, which makes it easy to carry your dog around.
- Ideal for containing a dog with serious separation anxiety.
- The best for traveling and camping. Due to its lightweight status, you can bring your dog along for road travels and even camping.
- It is very easy to store since it can be folded.

Disadvantages of soft-sided crates

- Hard to clean up in case of a major potty accident.
- Some dogs can chew their way out.
- Some dogs might figure out how to open the zip door.

4. Heavy-duty crates

These crates are designed using heavy-duty material. They are available in various styles and colors.

Advantages of heavy-duty crates

- There is almost a zero chance that the dog will break free.

- They are the most suitable for traveling by air.

Disadvantages of heavy-duty crates

- It is expensive, but keep in mind that they are made of sturdy material which justifies the expense.

5. Cute crates

As the name suggests, the cute crates are aesthetically pleasing, compared to the rest. They are mostly made of wood and exotic materials.

Advantages of cute crates

- It has a tasteful design.
- It is designed for comfort.

Disadvantages of cute crates

- Destructive dogs can chew at the wood

Chapter 4: The Importance of Exercise When Crate Training Your Puppy

Just like humans, dogs benefit from exercising as well. There are various exercises you may incorporate in your training regimen to strengthen your dog. Here are some of the benefits of putting your dog through exercises.

- **Bone health**

  When your dog does exercises like walking around, the muscles around his tendons will become strong. This improves his bone health and helps keep diseases at bay.

- **Heart health**

  Regular exercises will strengthen his heart. Exercising will increase the oxygen demands of his body, making his lungs more active. This will lead to optimal functioning lungs and heart, to keep up with the demands of his body. When he is constantly active, it minimizes the risk of developing heart complications.

- **Minimizes aggression**

  One of the many reasons why dogs may act aggressively is because they have pent-up energy. When they engage in various exercises, it is actually a way of letting go of the aggression, nervousness, and anxiety. They will be much more welcoming to strangers and critters.

- **Fights boredom**

  When your dog is bored, he is going to try to get your attention by whining and doing other things that you probably warned him against. However, he will feel entertained when you make him perform some exercises. When he is entertained, he is less likely to disturb you with whining or barking.

- **Improves metabolism**

Naturally, the metabolism of a dog can cater to some heavy-duty activities. When you make him perform exercises, you are actually enhancing the optimal function of his body. Exercising will enhance his metabolism rate.

- **Improves sleep**

   It is no secret that dogs love sleeping, but it can be hard for your dog to get quality sleep if he has been inactive throughout the day. When you make him perform some exercises, you will tire him out, and he will be able to get quality sleep. When a dog gets quality sleep, it helps his attitude. He becomes less aggressive and more receptive to the instructions of his owner.

- **Controls weight**

   The exercises help your dog burn calories which contribute to managing his weight. If your dog just consumes food and lies around, you can expect that he will gain weight. Gaining unnecessary weight could give rise to various health complications like heart disease.

- **Reduces separation anxiety**

Some dogs tend to develop a great bond with their owner, that they cannot ever withstand being separated. Exercising is one method of reducing the level of attachment that the dog has for his owner.

When you take him around for walks before you leave for work, it will trigger feelings of happiness in him, making him less inclined to whine or bark when you finally leave for work. Exercises will also tire him out and leave him wanting to sleep, making it easier for him to let you go to work.

- **Reduced chewing**
  Puppies are especially guilty of this habit. A puppy that is going through the teething phase tends to examine things with his mouth.

  Puppies have an overwhelming urge to chew at things. When you notice him doing it, you have to warn him that it is an inappropriate behavior.

  Warning him alone is not enough; the puppy will always get around to chewing more of your things. If you start putting him through routine exercises, his tendency of chewing at things will eventually fade away. The exercises will refresh him and make him calm.

- **Eliminate predatory behavior**
Your canine friend can have some serious predatory behaviors, which can make him harmful to either kids or critters. This is partly due to boredom and the pursuit of drama.

He could become hostile toward other people, and you would find yourself having to confine him and keep him away when guests come over. Exercising will make him spend his pent-up energy and put him in a good mood. He will be less inclined to treat others with hostility.

- **Increased agility**
Dogs naturally have to be agile to perform their activities. Since your puppy does not live in his natural habitat, you will have to devise ways of making him agile. Adding exercise to his routine is the most obvious way of ensuring that he is agile. You have to incorporate fun into the exercises and make them varied.

- **Prevents premature aging**

As an animal age, their lean muscle tends to diminish. If your dog just eats and sits around, he is likely to age at a faster rate compared to him being engaged in some exercises. A combination of good nutrition and routine exercises will promote the growth of lean muscle.

- **Get rid of toxins**

    When your puppy is inactive, he is at risk of accumulating toxic elements in his body. A sedentary lifestyle encourages harmful elements to build up inside his body. If he exercises, his body will function at an optimum level, which will lead to the elimination of toxic substances.

Chapter 5: What to do When Your Puppy is whining in the Crate

A puppy communicates his needs through cries, just like an infant. When you put your puppy in a crate, he will express his discomfort by crying, and it could take days for him to adjust to the new environment.

Whenever your puppy whines, be careful how you handle him because your response could affect his future behaviors. Here are some of the reasons that drive your puppy into whining and how to make him stop.

- **Sickness**

When your puppy whines all the time, it could be an indication that he is physically or emotionally unwell. Some of the symptoms to look out for include loss of appetite, diarrhea, lethargy, dizziness, vomiting, and shortness of breath.

If the puppy has bitten, licked, or scratched himself excessively around a certain area of his body, it is indicative of an infection, allergy, parasitic attack, and other skin issues.

If your puppy becomes withdrawn and recoils when you touch him, it is a sign that he is in a world of physical and emotional pain. When you discover any of these symptoms, you should take him to a vet for medical attention.

- **Loneliness**
  The puppy may be struggling with the separation from his parents. This results to whining as a way of sending out an alarm in case the mother can hear him and come to his rescue.

When you are dealing with an emotionally hurting puppy, the whining is usually low-pitched and never-ending. The best way to make him stop is to comfort him by making him see you a lot more. You can carry off the crate to a part of your house where you may interact with him while you are engaged in other things.

- **Fear**

  Various things about the new environment could trigger fear in your puppy. This will make your puppy whine. Inspect the crate and ensure there is nothing wrong. Also, reassure the puppy that everything is alright by stroking him and giving him treats.

- **Hunger**

  Your puppy could also whine due to hunger. Once you give him something to feed on, and he runs to the food like a rat to cheese, then you can be sure that it is hunger. If he ignores the food, it could mean something else is the cause of his discomfort.

- **Boredom**

  Another reason why the puppy could whine is due to boredom. Puppies love having a partner to play with to expend their energy. In the absence of a partner, toys will do. Get them a toy that piques their interest, and they will turn to it to fight the boredom away.

Here are more tips to make your puppy stop crying when you are not sure what the crying is all about:

- **Take him to the potty**

  Perhaps your puppy wants to relieve himself and is trying to get your attention. If he whines in the crate, carry him off to the potty. As soon as he relieves himself, carry him back into his crate without any distractions.

- **Play with him**

  Try to play with him and see how he reacts. This is likely going to get him into a good mood. Playing for a long duration will tire him out and make him want to sleep, which will put an end to his whining.

- **Put a sheet over the wire crate**

  In as much as wire crates are great for ventilation purposes, they are uncomfortable to a certain extent, especially during the night. Spreading a sheet over the wire crate will make your puppy feel more at ease, but you have to be careful in how you tuck away the ends because some puppies will not mind chewing at the sheet.

- **Bring the crate to your room**

If all your attempts to make him stop crying bear no fruits, you might as well consider bringing the crate into your room. This is certainly going to make him stop whining, especially when he is enveloped by your scent.

- **Discourage whining**

  A puppy is at an impressionable stage. You can use psychological tricks to modify his behavior.

  First of all, when he whines, make him stop and then praise him for not whining. You may give him treats and stroke him gently for not whining.

  Stop praising him and turn away when he whines. This will condition him to believe that he will only receive praise when he is not whining. Since he is at an impressionable stage, he will want to please you by doing what appears to make you happy.

Here are the two things not to do when your dog whines:

- Do not shout at him. In the worst case scenario, your puppy could misinterpret this as hostility and become scared. On the other hand, he could also perceive this as interest on your part and carry on with the whining, under the illusion that you are enjoying this activity too.

- Do not use a shock collar. A shock collar is a terrible way of making your dog stop whining. It could hurt him and make him resent being held in the crate.

Chapter 6: How to Handle Separation Anxiety When Crate Training Your Puppy

Dogs crave for their owner's attention. They hate it when their owner leaves them alone. For instance, when you leave for work your dog will probably make you feel guilty to look at you with pitiful eyes. Some other dogs will react more aggressively.

Dogs suffering from extreme separation anxiety will bark endlessly, try to ruin everything in their path, and relieve themselves around the house. In some cases, they may even injure themselves as they try to escape.

First of all, you have to establish whether your dog is suffering from separation anxiety or if he is just bored. When your dog is not getting stimulated enough, he can easily get bored and will resort to entertaining himself through barking and chewing at things.

You also have to find out whether your dog is exhibiting true separation anxiety or just 'learned' separation anxiety. Learned separation anxiety is caused by low self-control, and the behaviors that he exhibits are merely simulated. However, when a dog experiences true separation anxiety, he gets stressed whenever his owner is absent.

Signs of separation anxiety:

- Dedicating himself to destroying things
- Trying to get away from home while you are absent
- Relieving himself around the house even though he is potty trained
- Wearing pitiful eyes when you are about to leave the house
- Howling and barking during the day
- Purposely inflicting self-harm
- Acting clingy
- Barking and jumping when you finally come back home

Stop making a big deal out of leaving or arriving at home

Dog owners unknowingly trigger separation anxiety when they make a big deal of leaving or arriving home. Now, this makes your dog more conscious of your absence.

Ceremonial departures and arrivals can affect your dog's capacity to withstand your absence. When you have to leave for work in the morning, resist making a loud gesture that announces your intent to leave like grabbing car keys theatrically. When you come back, do not rush to pet him.

The power of exercise

Your dog has a lot of energy, and when he lacks a creative way of spending it, he might resort to raising hell and chewing at things. One of the best ways of spending your dog's energy is to take him out for a walk before you leave.

This exercise will relieve his anxiety and improve his mood and finally when you leave he will be too tired to complain. Introduce new challenges during the walk and make it as eventful as possible.

Leave behind a personal item with your puppy

Dogs have a strong sense of smell. They recognize your smell. When you leave behind a personal item of yours, the scent will remind your puppy of you. It will help comfort him whenever he feels unsafe. You may opt to leave behind a blanket or pillow.

The charm of toys

Nothing excites a puppy more than playtime. You could get him a puzzle toy to play with throughout the day.

Before you leave, give him a toy that challenges his skills. He will focus on the toy and have less time to mourn your departure.

Toys provide an escape from boredom as they cater to your puppy's need for stimulation. You might want to buy various puzzle toys to keep your puppy from getting bored.

Give him a different set of toys every day. Your departure will still be a bitter pill to swallow, but it will signify the start of games.

Be consistent

It can be difficult to establish a routine, especially where puppies are concerned, but it is a sure way of handling separation anxiety. When a dog settles into a routine, he is far less affected by your absence. Make him anticipate walking, feeding, playing and sleeping.

Take him to a daycare

Daycares are great for the social development of your dog. Find out a convenient daycare around your area of residence, and take him there. Track his development. Keep in mind that some dogs are terrified of populated areas.

Contact a dog behaviorist

If your dog is battling an extreme separation anxiety, consider taking him to a dog behaviorist and trainer. Tell him about your dog's tendencies and explore the various solutions available.

Chapter 7: What to do When Accidents Occur

The important thing is that you do not harm your dog. If you harm your dog because of an accident, he will associate the act with a negative feeling and next time he might do it at a more secluded area, where he thinks that you cannot find out.

Cleaning Urine

- **Paper towels**

  First, you ought to dry off the urine. A bunch of paper towels is great for wiping off the urine. With a gloved hand, press a bunch of paper towels or a rag onto the urine and clean the surface. If you have no gloves, you could use your foot, and this shields you against germs.

- **Carpet cleaner**

  Using paper towels are not enough, as the urine would dry off and there would be a conspicuous stain. Spray carpet cleaner on the urinated spot and wait for a few minutes to pass, then spray the carpet cleaner a second time and wipe the surface again. This will ensure that a stain will not develop afterward.

- **Baking soda**

  The urine of the dog harbors various germs. Baking soda is one of the most common household disinfectants. Sprinkle a generous amount of the baking soda over the spot and wipe it off. The baking soda not only destroys the activity of germs but also gets rid of the smell of the dog urine.

Cleaning Waste

Though it is common for a dog to urinate or waste separately, in some instances, he might both urinate and waste at the same time. Cleaning waste tends to be slightly more difficult.

- **Pick up the waste**
  Put gloves in your hands. Then hold open an inside-out grocery bag.

  Using a bunch of paper towels, grab as much waste off of the floor and put it in the inside-out grocery bag. When you are done collecting the waste, spray the floor with carpet cleaner to ensure that the waste does not dry off and give the room a terrible smell.

  Wipe the spray off the floor and sprinkle a generous amount of baking soda after a few minutes. The waste contains an army of germs. The baking soda is crucial in disinfecting your home surface as well as neutralizing the smell of the dog waste.

Tips on preventing accidents

Every dog owner has dealt with these kinds of accident. No matter how careful you are, your canine friend is going to surprise you from time to time. When an accident happens, you must act appropriately, so as not to you affect his future behavior.

Ensure that no medical issues are dogging him

Ensure that there are no medical issues that are limiting his capacity to control himself. When several accidents occur in a short amount of time, consider taking him to a vet office for a thorough health examination.

Some of the medical issues that trigger accidents include diarrhea, urinary tract infection, kidney stones, and bladder complications.

Interrupting his business

Dogs are very cunning, and when they have to relieve themselves, they crave some level of privacy. In most cases, you will be too late to remedy the situation.

However, there are some instances when you catch him in the middle of relieving himself or just before. In such instances, you have to intersect and lead him off to the appropriate spot.

Take him out more

When you make a habit of taking him out frequently, he will have more opportunity to relieve himself in the designated area. Depending on his age and breed, you can adjust the gaps between the breaks.

Make the effort of coming along instead of ordering him to go out alone. And when he displays appropriate potty manners, do not forget to praise him.

Puppies love to please their master, and when they associate their potty manners with making their master glad, they will be more inclined to upholding their potty manners. Track his progress and try to establish whether there is a pattern to his accidents.

Utilize the crate

It can be a bit tricky to ensure that there are no accidents while you are not watching. When you are sure that he is not going to relieve himself, you can let him wander through the house.

However, if he is going to be unattended for a long period of time, it is practical to confine him in a crate. Although, be sure not to confine him for much longer than he can handle.

Become more present

For the most part, an accident never occurs on willful commission. If there is no underlying medical issue, the accident may be as a result of a lapse in leadership. Your dog does not have a big brain. He has to be guided patiently and persistently until the system feels natural to him.

Chapter 8: Putting It Altogether – Creating a Crate training Plan that Works

Dogs have a natural denning instinct. Dog trainers advocate for crate training dogs so that they may have a safe and secure place to spend time and sleep, just as it would have been their natural setting.

Puppies need to be constantly watched. If they are left on their own, they will probably destroy valuable items and even endanger their lives. Since the dog owner is unlikely to have the whole day to spend with his puppy, the only viable option is to crate him.

With the right approach, you can introduce the crate to your puppy and make him appreciate being held in there. However, if you do not train him well he might despise the crate and attach negative feelings to the experience of being crated.

It is critical to crate your puppy because some of the benefits include:

- **Faster housetraining**
  A crate trained puppy takes well to housetraining. It can be distressing to have a puppy with bad potty manners, but crate training him will improve his capacity to control his bladder and bowel movement.

- **Protecting both him and your belongings**
  There are a lot of materials in your house that are potential health hazards to your puppy. You will be exposing him to these hazards when you let him roam around without your supervision.

  For instance, he could jump around and end up knocking down an object that may hurt him. Puppies love chewing at things. When you let him roam your house unattended, he will find a lot of items to chew on, thus ruining your belongings and not to mention that it may subject him to intestinal problems.

- **Comfort**

  Dogs love having a place of their own that they can retreat to when they want to be alone. The normal day can involve a lot of games, and he will eventually need to take a break from all the games and retreat to his improvised "cave." Whenever he feels threatened, he may run into his crate, and he will even spend the nights there as well.

- **Managing problems**

  Untrained puppies exhibit behaviors that are generally improper. It is upon the dog owner to show his puppy the acceptable way of behaving. Crate training your dog goes a long way in instilling healthy habits and by modifying his behaviors further. For instance, he will learn to answer your calls, rather than ignoring your commands.

- **Travel**

  Considering the hassles of traveling, it would be unwise to carry your puppy around. If you are traveling by road, it could pose various risks to him.

If you are traveling by air, authorities require that you use a crate. When you have your puppy confined in a crate, it becomes so much easier to handle him during travels.

When you buy the crate, ensure that it will meet the needs of your puppy. Consider the model and material of the crate that you buy, but above everything else, the crate should be just the right size to allow him to stand, sit down and turn around comfortably.

Introducing the crate

Never hold your puppy by the scruff of his neck and shove him into the crate. He will loathe every second he is held inside.

You have to figure out how to introduce the crate in a way that he will take a liking to it. First off, bribe him with treats and toys.

When you put a treat or a chewable toy inside, it will be enough incentive for your puppy to scurry into the crate. Leave the door open to show him that he can step out if he wants to.

Gradually, put the treats and the toys toward the farthest end so that he will have to walk all the way in. When he gets used to climbing into the crate, you can start closing the door and leaving him.

Start leaving him inside gradually, first for short moments and then for a prolonged amount of time. You have to come back from time to time to check on how he is doing, particularly to take him out so that he may relieve himself.

When a crate is properly used, the benefits are immense. However, some puppies can never cope with the fright of being contained in a crate and having their owner move away.

Such puppies should not be crated. Other instances when you should not hold your puppy in a crate include:

- **Escape attempts**
  If your puppy damages his crate in an attempt to escape, it is time to replace it or have it repaired.
- **Dampness**
  If the floor of the crate is damp, resist using that crate. The dampness is mostly caused by excessive salivation.
- **Accidents**
  When your dog defecates or urinates in the crate, you have to stop using it, at least until it is cleaned. Dogs have repetitive behaviors, and that

means they will be inclined to defecate on the spot that they previously defecated on.

- **Weather**

  Puppies get scared too easily. When the weather is terribly bad, you want to offer him reassurance. Have him stay close to you, instead of being on his own in his crate.

Chapter 9: Housetraining Using Crates

The purpose of housetraining is to instill discipline in your puppy and develop a close bond with him. To achieve the best results, you have to be persistent, patient and have a good attitude.

The amount of time needed to housetrain your puppy depends on some factors, but it takes from about a few months to a whole year for a puppy to be fully housetrained.

Begin early

Dog trainers suggest that you should begin to housetrain your puppy as soon as he is 12 weeks old. His ability to control his bladder and bowel movement begins to take shape around that age.

Get a crate

Puppies do not like soiling their private space. You have to get him a crate that fits his size, or else he is going to convert one side of the crate into his bathroom.

Teach him slowly that he must walk out to relieve himself. The best crate for him will depend on some internal and external factors. For instance, if it is very hot, you have to get him a crate that is ventilated.

Feeding schedule

Puppies love routines. When it comes to feeding, put him on a routine so that he is aware of his feeding time, and so that you may be able to distinguish his cycle of relieving himself. When it is not feeding time, take away the food. This will increase his level of self-control.

Pick a potty spot

Your puppy will be less inclined to soiling his crate if you provide a place where he will feel comfortable relieving himself. For instance, you could train him to relieve himself on a small area of your yard.

It becomes easy to build up on that behavior because puppies like relieving themselves on the exact same area they did before. This does not mean that you have automatically eradicated all possibility of an accident.

With patience and persistence, you can make his potty manners excellent.

Taking him out

One thing you have to understand about puppies is that they adore being guided by the owner. Until they are trained properly, they cannot take initiative.

You will have to take him out for the most part of housetraining. In the morning, the first thing is to check up on the little guy, and take him out to relieve himself.

During the day, you can start taking him out at 30-minute intervals, and then increase it to an hour. When he clears a meal, wait for a short moment and then take him out.

You should also take him out every time he wakes up from a nap. Before you put him back in his sleeping abode at night, ensure that he relieves himself.

Praise him

Puppies are very sensitive and are always in need of their owner's attention. There is no better way of showering him with attention, than a reward for his good deeds.

For instance, when he exhibits excellent potty manners, praise him. He is going to want to keep up his manners so that he can please you, and earn praise from you in return. Also, it will foster a great bonding experience when you praise him.

Set up an area for playing

Younger puppies require to be taken out more frequently than older ones. You should never keep your puppy confined in his crate for more than six hours during the day.

You can ask someone else to take them out if you are not around or you may want to drop them off at a daycare. If that is not entirely possible, you have to create a place where he will be free to play.

Place everything he requires around that playing area and leave him alone with the knowledge that his mess will be easy to clean up, as it will be restricted to that area alone.

Learn the signs

Puppies cannot express their needs like a human being, but there are still cues to watch out for to inform you what he wants. When he is not feeling good, he will display behaviors such as whining, barking, circling, and sniffing. You have to go and take him out.

Puppies get scared

When you take him out to relieve himself at night, hang around until he actually does it. Puppies are very sensitive and have a tendency of getting scared especially if the weather is bad.

When they are scared, it limits their capacity to relieve themselves. You will want to offer him security and make sure that he is relieving himself.

Some people who leave their puppy alone outside often find that the puppy ends up relieving himself inside the house instead. He was probably too scared to do it outside.

The key to housetraining a puppy is supervision. If you are too busy to supervise him, you have to consider getting help.

Chapter 10: Feeding Your Dog in the Crate

Devising a great diet plan for your puppy is a big task. Dog trainers warn against creating variety because it could harm his digestion.

You have to throw any leftover food and ensure that the bowls have water throughout the day. The diet requirements for puppies are much more intense than the requirements for older dogs because puppies are physically developing at a massive rate.

To come up with a perfect diet plan, you have to conduct your research and even seek help from the breeder.

First-year timeline

- **6 – 12 weeks**

  Puppy food is all their bodies can withstand. If you give them adult food, it could harm their vulnerable digestive system, not to mention that there would probably be a case of nutrition deficiency. Ideally, the puppy should be fed around four times each day.

- **3 – 6 months**

  At this stage, the puppy's body is taking shape, and you may slightly reduce the amount of food.

- **6 – 12 months**

  Gradually make the switch from puppy food into adult food. You can feed him twice a day.

Dry foods

There is a wide selection of dry foods in the market. You have to buy the food that is tailored for your puppy.

The best food for your puppy depends on various factors like the key ingredients it contains, and the price it costs. However, the most expensive dry foods contain the highest concentration of nutrients.

Semi-moist and tinned foods

The quality depends on the price range. But you have to stick with ingredients that work for your puppy. Buy complete foods as opposed to foods that require you to make additions.

Treats

The best treats should have a great taste and at the same time, cater to a dog's dietary needs. Treats should be given economically. Some treats may contain lots of milk products, sugar, colorings, fat and even chemicals, so you have to find treats that will not affect your puppy.

Selecting high-quality puppy food

Your puppy's nutrition needs are high. Before you purchase any foods, you first have to do your research and analyze the foods carefully. You can solicit advice from vet officers and the breeder.

And when you introduce a type of food to your puppy, always study how your puppy reacts. If he appears allergic to it, you have to stop giving him more of that food.

How to determine whether the puppy food will meet your puppy's needs

The nutritional guidelines that most pet food manufacturers follow are set by the American Feed Control Officials. Always check if the package label states that the food is AAFCO-compliant. The label should also indicate the stage of the puppy that the food is meant for.

How much should you feed your puppy?

Puppies are in a state of rapid growth in their first five months. To keep up with their caloric demands, you should serve them a generous amount of food. You can be guided by the feeding charts on product labels. They recommend appropriate amounts of food basing on the age and weight of the puppy.

Knowing whether your puppy is feeding well

Vet officers examine the state of a puppy using the body conditioning score, which ranges from one to five, with one standing for emaciated, and five standing for obesity. A healthy puppy should clock two.

What kind of foods can harm your puppy?

Some of the foods that people eat can have harmful effects on your puppy. These foods include raisins, grapes, avocados, macadamia, bread, garlic, onion, dairy products, coffee, alcohol, gum, and candy.

Puppy feeding tips

- **Understand the nutritional content**
  Always examine the nutritional value of the dog food.
  Some ingredients may be doing more harm than good
  to your dog. To be clear about the appropriate
  ingredients, you may want to seek guidance from the
  breeder.

- **Do not feed him the moment you come home**
  Feeding him as soon as you arrive will trigger an
  emotional message and encourage attachment.
  Therefore, his separation anxiety will increase.

  Arrange for him to be fed on a schedule. If you arrive
  with a fanfare, you are going to make him emotional,
  and he will not be okay with you leaving him again.

  Instead, when you arrive home, you may want to do
  some other activity first before you come back to him,
  but if you must attend to him first, it should be
  nothing more than petting and playing around.

- **Consult a vet officer before changing your
  puppy's diet**

Putting your puppy under a variety of diets will give rise to digestion complications. Consult your veterinary officer and also the breeder if you have to change your puppy's diet.

- **Create the right environment for having meals**
Never try to take away your puppy's food while he is eating. This could trigger his food aggression and complicate his overall behavior.

- **Meal timing**
Do not feed your puppy before he travels by car. Otherwise, he will experience car sickness. Also, do not feed him shortly before or after exercising as this would lead to bloating.

- **Do not encourage begging**
Never feed your dog from the table, as this will encourage him to start seeking your attention through begging.

- **Plenty of water**
Puppies have a serious need for water. You should station bowls of clean water in their crates and also at strategic positions around their playing area.

Their water consumption goes up during the summer. You should consider increasing the number of bowls.

Chapter 11: Steps to Prevent Whining and Barking

Barking and whining are the two common ways that your dog communicates his needs, but it can be irritating when your dog barks or whines nonstop. The key towards preventing your dog from barking himself hoarse is to ensure that you have eliminated all scenarios that would encourage barking.

Here are some of the tips for preventing your dog from whining and barking:

Check on him regularly

Puppies are in need of constant attention. If you go for a long time without checking up on him, you risk making him relieve himself where he should not, as well as whine and bark incessantly.

You should especially keep an eye on him if you know that he is recently fed. Realize that puppies do not have a lot of control over their bladders or bowel movement and they will relieve themselves at the slightest inclination.

When you check up on him regularly, it will be easy to find out his needs, and make him comfortable. You are also able to guide him to the appropriate location to relieve himself.

If he is the type that gets scared easily, your constant presence will help him adjust to the environment and will get rid of his anxiety.

Get the appropriate crate size

What is the appropriate crate size? One that allows him to stand, sit down, turn around, and get through the door without a hassle.

Most dog owners make the mistake of buying a crate that is a few sizes too big. If you are going to leave him inside the crate for a prolonged period of time, understand that he will walk up to one side of the crate and relieve himself.

A crate is not the best place for relieving himself. Dogs hate sleeping in an area that has been soiled.

The excrement will attract all sorts of bad bacteria, which will harm your dog. Under such circumstances, your dog will develop an inclination towards barking and whining.

When you acquire the right size of a crate, it will encourage him to develop appropriate potty manners, therefore, keeping his abode safe and clean.

Take him for bathroom breaks regularly

Your dog does not have a mouth to speak for himself. You will have to train him so that he may get along with you.

When you make him overstay behind closed doors, you are only asking that he relieves himself there. Get into the habit of taking him to his potty.
When he relieves himself appropriately, praise him verbally and give him a treat. He will associate proper potty manners with receiving a treat.

This will eliminate chances of accidents, as well as stabilize your dog's emotional state so that he will refrain from barking and whining.

Eliminate distractions

Dogs have very developed senses. They can perceive things and people long before you do.

For instance, a dog might become aware of an approaching person long before you will, and resort to barking. It could seem like he is barking for no reason at all until the person gets into your line of sight.

When you eliminate distractions, you will create an enabling environment for your dog to relax, and focus on his activities. You have to be especially careful where you position his crate.

Ideally, you should place the crate in an open and quiet area. If there are distractions, like kids playing, the dog is likely to respond with incessant barking.

It does not necessarily mean that he is scared. He might be making a cry of glee and is probably asking to get involved in the fun.

Distractions also limit the capacity of your puppy to relieve himself. If you take him out to relieve himself and he is distracted, he might not actually do it, he will most likely go back in the house and relieve himself.

Feed him well

A dog could bark and whine as a result of experiencing hunger. You do not have to wait until he starts complaining about food.

Create a feeding schedule. Dogs love schedules. And ensure that he gets fed when the time is due. The right combination of food, toys, and sleep will elevate your canine friend to untold levels of ecstasy.

Socialize him

Dog owners seem to think that socializing a dog involves taking him to a daycare. That is a great method of socializing, but it is quite expensive.

How about letting him play with other pets and kids? This will make him less aggressive and more welcoming to people, and critters. His instinctual barks will decrease and possibly even disappear altogether.

Medical checkups

Most dog owners wait until it is obvious that their puppy is in need of medical attention. When you are attentive, the early signs are enough to spur you into action.

Taking a puppy for a medical checkup will ensure that you keep the illnesses at bay. When your puppy is healthy, it will be unlikely he will cry and complain.

Chapter 12: Crate Training Your Dog for Travel

If you are traveling and you intend to bring your puppy along, ensure that he is contained in an appropriate crate, in case he gives you a rough time. If you are traveling by air, your crate must be IATA-compliant.

If you are driving, always confine your puppy for his safety. A crate allows the puppy to have his own space in which he can feel safe.

When he is taken out to a new location, he is unlikely to get scared. Crate training your puppy is really important when traveling, as it lets your puppy have their own space and allows you to set boundaries.

Prepare early enough

You should start preparing as soon as you know that you are traveling. Buy the right size and do your research when purchasing a dog crate.

Ensure that you have taken the measurements of your dog. The crate must be big enough to allow him to stand, sit down and turn around comfortably.

The crate should be made of heavy-duty plastic with a metal grill door. Latches, clips, and dials should be made of sturdy material.

The crate should also be properly ventilated and has bedding. When you start crate training your puppy early enough, he will get used to his new space, and will not give you trouble during the travel.

Normalize the travel crate

Encourage your puppy to get inside by putting treats and toys in the crate. Start feeding your puppy inside the crate so that he can get used to it.

When he gets familiar with the crate, he will start going in and out on his own will and even develop an attachment to his personal space.

Start closing the door for a short period of time and then gradually extend the time, and then put the crate in the car and drive over short distances so that he may feel what it is like to be driven around.

Here are some of the reasons why it is crucial to crate train your dog while preparing for a journey.

- **Makes traveling easier**
  Traveling with your dog unrestrained can be very hectic and dangerous. Puppies have high energy. They will keep moving around, and you will have to constantly watch them in case they hurt themselves. If you are traveling by air, it beats logic not to confine your canine friend.

- **Good behavior**
  A crate trained dog is responsive to commands than an untrained dog. A crate trained dog will exhibit the best manners during the journey and will not be difficult to control.

On the other hand, an untrained dog would be difficult to handle and is likely to behave in a manner that you disapprove of. For instance, you might call him, and he refuses to come.

- **Reduces damage**

  When you confine your canine friend, you restrict him from engaging in various activities which can cause damage. Chewing is one of the pastimes of puppies that usually results in damage.

  Your puppy has no regard to your valuable items so he will gnaw even at costly items like shoes and furniture.

- **Safety**

  If you are traveling by car, he is safe in his private space. If you are traveling by air, confining your canine friend would keep him safe, considering that it is easy to lose him to the crowd.

- **Helps him settle in a new location**

  When you move to a new location, it will be easier for your puppy to adjust because he still has his private space.

- **Allows you to enjoy your journey**

  Driving while watching your puppy at the same time, can be dangerous and can ruin the experience. If you confine him to his crate, it relieves you of the worry, and you can enjoy your journey.

- **Bad weather**

  Puppies are scared of going out when the weather is bad. It scares them so much that they sometimes become unable to relieve themselves. However, when they are confined to their crates, they tend to get over their anxiety quicker.

Chapter 13: How Long Does it Take to Crate Train Your Puppy?

Getting a new dog has its challenges. The dog has to adapt to a new environment and has to deal with being separated from his former family.

As the dog owner, you may want to spend the whole day with your dog, but it is unrealistic because you need to go to work. Considering that your puppy is going to stay in the house for a long period of time while you are away, it is practical to confine him in a crate.

Crating your puppy is not meant to be a form of cruelty, but some dog owners make the mistake of letting the puppies stay in their crates for a long period of time. When a puppy is held in a crate for a prolonged amount of time, he is likely to develop anxiety and depression, and he will become vulnerable to certain illnesses due to the lack of exercise.

Crate training during the day

Puppies are active during the day. The appropriate amount of time that you can leave your puppy inside the crate is informed by his age and his ability to control both his bladder and bowel movement.

According to the ASPCA, a puppy that is no more than eight weeks old should not be held in a crate for longer than an hour. When he crosses the eight-week old threshold, you may gradually increase the amount of time that you confine him in the crate.

From 14 to 16 weeks old, you can hold him in the crate for three to four hours. For puppies that are 17 weeks old and beyond, you should not confine them for more than six hours. Regardless of his age, you should never hold him in his crate longer than he can control his bladder and bowel movement.

Crate training at night

If your puppy has developed an attachment to his crate as most puppies do, he will love nothing more than retiring to his "den" after jumping around throughout the day. At night he will be asleep and obviously much less active than during the day, but still, you have to awaken to take him out if he cannot control his bladder or bowel movement throughout the night.

Crate training while you are at work

Most people crate train their puppies simply because they cannot afford to be around the whole day to watch him. A crate allows them to keep their puppy safe while they go to work.

A puppy must not be left in the crate for more than five hours. If you work near your home, you have to come back at appointed times to take him out.

If that is not possible, then consider enlisting the services of another person to help you. Keeping your puppy in the crate for a prolonged time can trigger depression and anxiety. If you cannot find another person to take him out, you need to construct a playing section within the house where your puppy can have free reign throughout the day.

Chapter 14: When Should You Stop Crate training Your Puppy?

A crate provides security and shelter for your puppy, and it also allows the owner to be at peace. Dog trainers' advocate for all dogs to be crate trained.

Crating saves the dog owner a lot of trouble, especially when it comes to the chewing habit of most puppies. Puppies tend to chew at things, even though they could be expensive things like shoes and expensive mats.

There also comes a time where you have to stop crating the dog. It all depends on the dog in question and the circumstances of the dog owner.

His personality

Assume that you have two dogs of different breeds. One of the dogs tends to lie down and stay in one place for an extended amount of time, while the other dog loves to jump around and chew up things.

In this case, it is alright to stop crating the first dog, but you should continue crating the second dog, in case he ruins valuable items. When your dog consistently demonstrates that he is up to no harm, then he can be trusted to be by himself.

However, if your dog has high-energy and adrenaline, the worst mistake you can do is leave him by himself while you are away.

Extreme separation anxiety

If your dog has proven incapable of handling being alone, you might as well consider putting him off the crate. This will make him at peace.

When a dog is first put in the crate, the obvious reaction is rebellion. He ends up rebelling against his new home for a certain period of time, then he adapts to his new environment.

Sadly, some dogs never seem to adjust to living in the crate. It is actually a form of torture when you leave them there under the assumption that they will eventually come into terms with it.

When you find out that your dog cannot handle the anxiety that comes with being separated from you, you might want to look for an alternative to crating. When you are absent, he may exhibit behaviors like whining and barking endlessly.

He is housetrained

A housetrained dog will exhibit appropriate potty manners. He will resist defecating indoors as he is aware that it annoys you. It would be okay to stop crating such a dog.

When he knows all that is expected of him, you will not have to run around after him to ensure that he does not stray. A housetrained dog exhibits pleasant manners. He understands the various actions by him that would upset you and tries not to do them.

Does not chew

The problem of chewing items is much more pronounced in puppies than older dogs. Puppies are going through the initial stages of teething.

Puppies explore their surrounding using their mouth, and they find chewing things almost irresistible. If you are not careful, your puppy could chew expensive things and set you many thousands back.

It is also a dangerous habit, considering that the material he chews might affect his digestive system and give rise to all sorts of complications. This habit of chewing things persists even beyond the initial stages of a dog.

When you guide your dog into understanding that chewing things is not okay, he would eventually drop the habit. If your dog has gotten rid of the habit, it is okay not to crate him.

You can let him roam around the house, knowing too well that he will not be tempted to chewing your things again.

Bad weather

If you live in an area with hostile climatic conditions, you should discontinue crating your dog. For instance, if your region suddenly becomes hot, it would be cruel to still keep your dog in his crate, as his temperature would rise and the limited ventilation of the crate will not help matters.

Similarly, if your area of residence suddenly grew cold, you should keep him out of the crate as the cold would get to him. During stormy seasons, your dog gets too scared, and you might want to reassure him by having him stay close to you.

Medication

When you take your dog to the vet office, he might receive treatment that will make him very vulnerable. The doctor might advise against putting him in the crate until he gets well.

Chapter 15: Common Problems You Might Run Into

Crate training your dog is not a walk in the park. It takes patience and persistence to achieve the results that you desire. In the end, it pays off as you have a well-behaved dog. Here are some of the challenges you might run into while crate training:

Chewing

Puppies are particularly guilty of this habit. Since they explore the world around them using their small mouths, puppies often chew up things.

He might go around searching for things to chew as a way of calming himself. This is a major challenge because he will often chew at valuable things.

If you contain him in a plastic crate, he might also start chewing the plastic material in an attempt to break free from the confinement. This habit of chewing things does not just make you lose things, but also it poses serious health concerns to the puppy.

The material that he chews could affect the normal function of his intestines. You do not have to fight away this habit, but rather offer him guidance on the chewable and non-chewable things.

You can achieve this by introducing chewable toys. This will allow him to indulge his natural instinct of gnawing at things, albeit in a safe and fun way. If you catch him chewing things that he should not, just warn him sternly against repeating the mistake.

Not coming when you call him

It can get frustrating when your dog fails to heed your calls. Whenever you call to him, and he ignores you, never assume that he has acquired a snobbish attitude without first establishing what is causing him to ignore you.

Also, do not get mad at him or even worse, do not hurt him. Always praise your dog whenever he comes to you.

This will make him associate the action of coming to you with getting praised. If your dog is still unresponsive to your calling him, do not run after him. Instead, take backward steps as you call on him and if it still does not work, order him to sit and go get him.

Separation anxiety

Dogs quickly establish bonds with their owners. Some dogs are good at withstanding being alone while others are not so good.

Puppies are particularly needy. Separation anxiety in a puppy is triggered the moment he sees that you are about to leave him, which scares him.

Reassure your puppy that everything is alright, and you will be back soon. Get him a chewable toy that he can play with while you are not around. Make sure that you do not make a big deal of leaving or coming back home, as it will intensify his feelings of attachment.

Whining

Puppies love expressing their needs through whining. It can be especially exhausting when your puppy will not keep quiet, especially at the night.

There are various reasons why a puppy whines, it could be a medical issue, getting scared, separation anxiety, hunger, boredom, or as a way of seeking attention. When your puppy whines do not yell at him, as it could scare him and make him withdraw.

Try to establish what is troubling your puppy and if you cannot come around it, then consider taking him to a vet for a checkup.

Barking at the door

On the occasion that your puppy is pumped enough, he might graduate from mere whining and start barking. This is usually a way of getting your attention.

For instance, your puppy could be uncomfortable with being held in the crate, and he could bark incessantly as a way of expressing his rebelliousness. Ceaseless barking might also be indicative of an awaiting threat.

Try to establish whether there is a foreign object inside his crate that is scaring him. If the barking is so extreme that neighbors come to complain about it, you might want to take your puppy for a checkup and maybe put him on medication.

Biting

Your dog could develop a tendency of biting – either people or critters. This indicates a level of distrust.

Focus on making him as comfortable as can be when he is around other people. You can achieve this by developing his social skills.

For instance, you may take him to a daycare and let him socialize with his kind. This will make him more welcoming to other people and other pets.

When your dog has a problem with biting, it could limit your social life, as some people might get scared of being near him.

Accidents

In most cases, accidents are as a result of poor leadership on the part of the dog owner. But all in all, accidents are to be expected.

Do not hurt or yell at your dog, such reactions would scare him and make him scout for a more private area to relieve himself next time. Understand that puppies need to be shown the same thing over and over again.

With enough practice, his potty manners will eventually become fitting. Another major cause of accidents is medical problems.

If your puppy has diarrhea, he will not be able to control his bowel movement. If his urinary tract is infected, he will not be able to control his bladder.

Find out whether he is allergic to some of the foods that you are giving him, and if you cannot understand the triggers of the accident, it is time to take him to the vet for a checkup.

Conclusion

Subtly introduce the crate to your puppy. For instance, you can put a treat in the crate and place the puppy near the entrance.

He is likely to scurry in and devour the treat. When he gets in do not be too quick to shut the door, but rather give him some time to explore the crate.

Dogs have a natural denning instinct, and they adore the solitude that crates give them. If he appears satisfied with the crate, you can shut the door and move away.

Gradually increase the amount of time that you leave him in the crate, but always ensure that you take him out so that he can relieve himself. When selecting the crate for your puppy, you have to ensure that it fits him perfectly.

He should be able to stand up, sit down, and turn around comfortably. If the crate is too big, he might convert one end of the crate into his potty and the other end as his sleeping quarters.

Always guide your puppy with patience and persistence until he acquires all the habits that you deem appropriate.

Made in the USA
Middletown, DE
07 February 2020